My Miracle

Based on a True Story

Rodney Barnes

authorHOUSE®

AuthorHouse™
1663 Liberty Drive, Suite 200
Bloomington, IN 47403
www.authorhouse.com
Phone: 1-800-839-8640

First published by AuthorHouse 2/23/2009

ISBN: 978-1-4389-5524-7 (sc)

Printed in the United States of America
Bloomington, Indiana

This book is printed on acid-free paper.

Contents

Introduction
Looking at Life

The way your life is at the present moment, are you ready to face what tomorrow may hold?

The swings in our lives move like the swings at a park, they are flexible. They can move, but they can also stop. It's nice to have that swing go as high as you can move it. It shows what life is capable of offering. At the age of one we cannot even get on the swing, having no idea how. As we get older, we become able, but at an elderly age, we once again cannot. Capabilities are what we learn as our age increases, but we lose them when we reach a certain point in our lives.

In a way, that's a good thing, only because people can learn from each other. The older generation can go on for hours and hours, just talking about earlier years in this world. When they talk about the past, it fills their future with hope. It can also bring back moments in which they might have been proud of themselves. Seeing that their hearts do not have much more opportunity for self-fulfillment is sad.

People should be able to speak their minds and take that chance at life. It's called freedom. This encourages younger generations to think, strive, complete, or be successful for themselves, seeking their chance to be the people they want to be.

Some people can express their thoughts and feelings. Some people can even express themselves in a way that can deeply touch another person. They might have this gift hiding inside of them and not even know it. All it takes is a touch. It can bring out the best in us.

However, I never took the time to put it all together, until now. I personally know how hard life can be. By yourself, it can be a struggle to see through the darkness. At that time, I could not see anything in existence that could slow me.

It now bothers me to think that some people need to wait for an event in their lives to see the light or find a quest. In fact, all it takes is a blink of an eye, and a change can affect your whole future. There are times when we are not ready, not wanting to adjust, or when we think it can't happen to us. The reality is that life experiences can, do, and will occur.

The question is, are you ready for that moment to make a difference in your life? This moment is the possibility to adjust to the future. What if you are not focused, involved, or concerned about that question? Despite your self-absorption, such an event like this could be heading your way.

I was told in the past that God works in mysterious ways, but what do these words mean? How can a person use these five words to enhance his or her life? What if you do not follow or even believe in God. In any case, how far can your current outlook of life take you? It's what you put into life that comes out.

The simple fact is that we all follow what works best for us. The words "best for us" underline what we will become, not knowing what lies ahead. We really don't know what's on the other side or what might happen down the road. I do know this, however: what is earned in trust can be given back. If you ever wonder regarding your outcome, then your outcome should be in the trust you have earned.

The changes and roads we all arrive at in our lives can either break us or make us even stronger, and the time limits are unpredictable. It is sad when it takes a person a long time to find their way. It is depressing when a person is not even given that chance, either by age or accident. That is why I hope that this story can be helpful to you, because finding your destiny or being comfortable is a positive direction and the only way to prevail.

Chapter 1
My Early Years

My name is Rodney. I was born in St. Petersburg, Florida, on August 19, 1970. I was the youngest of the family, and the only Florida native among us. That was because my family had taken a vacation to Florida from Ohio and never turned back. My life growing up was full of the love of others. We had everything a soul needed to survive.

Yes, I'm proud to have the most glorious, encouraging, outstanding, and understanding parents in the world, Harold and Virginia. My brother and sister always shared their love with me. Jeff was the oldest and Lisa was stuck in the middle. Having these gifts always kept a smile on my face.

My Childhood

I lived in a humble, warm, sincere home. My dad remodeled our house to make it more suitable for the entire family.

The family always went overboard giving a hand to anybody who was in need. We all lived in a nice neighborhood with friendly faces. From my childhood on, I was lucky to be surrounded by friends. Being a people person was handed down from the roots of the family. It was just natural for me to be around others.

We were the richest people on this earth, in my mind. My mother was everything that I needed her to be. She would go out of her way to make sure that I was happy in every way, and she very much enjoyed being around us kids. She still loves us to this day.

Dad was my dad. I loved him for who he was. He was very strong at whatever he put his mind to. My dad was an inspiration for me to learn along the way. His work ethics taught me to be responsible. He is the cause of my ability to perform anything that I put my mind to. I looked up to my dad.

As for my brother and sister, they gave me inspiration. Being the youngest, I learned what not to do and what to achieve from them. They also showed me the possibilities of what I could become and how to live my life. For this, I simply watched and learned from afar.

In the early years, being a part of the family was being together as a family. We would share because sharing was who we were. Everyone had their own responsibilities to our home. Everyone fulfilled that degree of partnership. Along the way, both of my parents' families were a part of our relationship. We had good times and enjoyed life. We would also gather together to explore some interesting retreats or events.

My goal was to complete whatever I had started. I did this because it was in my blood, but also it made me happy. Each member of my family took on exciting challenges because it made us stronger and developed our leadership skills. We very much enjoyed being active in several sports.

One example was that the family (including my dad's part of the family) had started a bicycle racing team. It was called the "Barnes Stormers." I loved racing bikes as a child. It had been a common end of mine to finish first before the other youth. I still have a couple of trophies from nineteen seventy- seven. The other young mates did try to cross the finish line first. Sometimes they did overpower us; we must have had a problem with the bike.

There was a bicycle track in Clearwater, Florida, which is now a baseball field. It had a hill that you had to start on. First you had to line up in numbers along a wooden platform that was about a foot high and a few feet across. All of the racers would stand up on their pedals with their bikes against a gate, waiting for it to drop. As soon as it did, all of the bike racers would descend the hill. Then we'd race around turns and hit jumps to see who would take the lead. The track would have these big turns, with big and small jumps in a row, and there were oblivious family members yelling, "Go, go, go" from the side.

A couple of people would tangle up and crash, hitting the hard clay. All of my dad's side of the family and friends would go all over town to different tracks to race competitively. There must have been ten to twenty kids racing on our team. As the years continued to move forward, more possibilities arose, and slowly, the families would all develop different interests.

Dad had soon found a new career, paving asphalt. It was a good job that brought us a higher income. My mom's side of the family was already involved in this. During those years, all of my uncles and a couple of my aunts were in the asphalt paving business.

My relatives had sharp-looking dump trucks and trailers. They were painted with style and had a bright shine to them. They treated the trucks, trailers, and equipment with respect because it was the equipment that put food on the table and money in our pockets.

My pops had a reputation for getting the job done right. Not long after getting caught up in the paving business, we got our own transportation and equipment. All of the families would travel around together, going to these little country towns. We would get jobs with commercial and residential businesses. My mom, sister, and I would catch up with my dad and the relatives and spend the whole summer with them until school started again.

It was a nice retreat, getting away from my home, because it was peaceful and really beautiful out in these country towns. I liked the mountains, cool weather, and animals that were not far away.

My brother had just been issued his driver's license around this time, and Dad made him use it! He had to drive our dump truck for miles and miles because there weren't asphalt plants in every little town. When he returned to the job site, it was time to pave. The dump truck and a spreader box would do their part, with help from the older guys.

After laying the asphalt, it would need to be pressed down. That's when I would step in. Dad would sometimes let me drive the roller. You would have to drive either frontward or backward the whole distance without stopping so that you wouldn't leave a line indented in the driveway. When the rolling was done, the job was done.

After a few years of asphalt paving, my family got out of the business. I don't really know what had caused this. I never asked what the reason was, but I still have some relatives that are in this business. They still find satisfaction in their work. With these years of experience, they continue to add to their knowledge.

During the early years of school my parents enrolled me in a Catholic school. Getting into trouble and even failing in the public school system led to this rearrangement. I started this new school in the second grade. As I spent the years at this school I was somewhat devoted, but not much. This style of religion worked for others, but not me.

I acted out a performance that was given to me. I don't even recall having a relationship with God. This school had quickly straightened out my academic future. It was a fulfilling experience that lasted all the way up to the end of my fifth-grade year.

At that age, my brother and sister also went to this school for a few years. My whole family took part in the Catholic lifestyle. We were involved in all of the activities. The Catholic families and other people who did not attend the church were delighted about being a part of the events and the fair. It was great when the fair had come around. There had been some cool rides.

By now, I was prepared for the public school system. After I departed from this school to enter the sixth grade, the Catholic lifestyle slowly became different for all of us. As my years passed by, so did this church. It became dimmer and dimmer. The events and the fair, they all just vanished. I'm not accusing anyone at all; it was no one's fault.

Chapter 2
Years Adding On

Now, as for the clock, it quickly moves forward in my life. With years passing by, we all grew up so soon. Jeff had tied the knot in his late teens. He married his longtime sweetheart, Sandy. They were a match from the start. I was very pleased for both of them, but Lisa and I were nowhere near that point in our lives. We were not ready for that kind of commitment.

Jeff had started stock racing as a hobby about the same time he got married. He liked going fast. Sandy loved being a part of racing because her family was also interested in this sport. It seemed like everybody we knew went to a track called Sunshine Speedway, either to race or watch. The track was not far from where I lived. As a matter of fact, the entire Barnes family had been active in racing for years. Dad and one of his brothers, Ernie, were very good. They had been involved in drag racing up in Ohio, and then after moving to Florida, they got into stockcar racing.

As for going fast, time on this planet rotates with speed just like our lives rotate. And, people on this planet sometimes just cannot hold on. The rotation just gets too fast to withstand. One part in the rotation was just too fast for me. I didn't realize the speed. All of a sudden, my parents were heading in the wrong direction.

For some reason, their relationship was not working and talk of a divorce slowly began with my mom and dad. We kids took their divorce pretty hard. It was so difficult because we had never imagined that this would happen in our family. Sure, you would see others divorce, but your own parents? That was something that was difficult for me to swallow. I had assumed that my parents got along great. I had no way of seeing inside their hearts. I could not repair the part that was damaged or even see inside their emotions. They were doing a good job of it on the outside. However, that was something I had to live with, another part of life.

That's why you have to try to keep yourself afloat. I must have been fifteen years old. I was just trying to do my thing, overlook it, while keeping my head up and staying afloat. My life was surfing, skating, partying, finding girls and trouble, and, before I forget, working—those were my alternatives.

It didn't take long for my dad to remarry. Her name was Beverly, and she seemed to be a very nice person. I don't know much about how the two of them got together. I never held a grudge towards them. When I got to know her, she turned out to be an awesome step-mom. It was just obvious that Dad hadn't waited long to move forward. On the other hand, it took my mother years to get married. She had dated this guy named Steve for fourteen years before they tied the knot. During that time he was good to her, and that was good enough for me.

Around the first year of my mother dating Steve is when I got my best furry little friend. Steve got together with a personal friend who had the same breed of dog that he did, and, within a few months, my puppy was born. It was a black-and-tan, short-haired Rottweiler. He was so adorable. We all agreed on the name Fritz. As this little adorable puppy got older, I loved wrestling with him, especially in the backyard. He would always respond to victory by licking me all over my face and ears. He became my dearest, best buddy. I loved that dog very much.

Finally, high school was a done deal. I had graduated from Gibbs High in St. Petersburg, Florida. That was a jewel in itself. Finishing high school was probably my greatest achievement at the time and some of the family had been present to enjoy this celebration.

My graduation w/ Mom and Sister

I loved standing up on that pedestal. No more studying, taking notes or going to those classes—it was over!

It was an ultimately satisfying feeling, throwing my cap into the air along with the other classmates and my friends at school, but saying good-bye to my special teachers (the ones who had made testing easier) wasn't that cool!

During the senior year, I decided on going into the military. I wanted so badly to enlist in the armed forces and serve my country. The military seemed to offer me an opportunity to be a great role model for this country. After getting in touch with a recruiter, I went in to take the test. I thought that everyone passes this test, but that wasn't the case. I did not pass it. I thought that maybe I had read it wrong. So, I went in again to take it, and sure enough, it was the same result.

Since the military hadn't worked out, I thought maybe it was back to school for me. A good percentage of my friends were going. Some of my friends had already gone off to bigger colleges and universities. My first move was to find out what I needed to do. I hadn't taken any college courses in high school. So, I had to take the pretest to even see where I stood.

I went to St. Petersburg Junior College and spoke to a counselor. Afterwards, I could see that making all of the arrangements and taking the test was not for me. I couldn't see myself taking more classes and tests. There were parties, girls, and, before I forget, work. I liked the first two the most. As for the jobs, they were easy to find. I never got fired, which was a good thing!

Friday nights, I would just socialize with friends. We would sometimes go to the beach at night, being inclined to play volleyball, hit the dance clubs, and spend time over at a friend's house. My friends and I knew how to have a good time. We would always try something new that caught our attention! There was one thing that always went along for the ride. We liked drinking that other fizzy stuff, beer.

Not just me, but everyone else as well thought that it was a top priority. Yes, I was underage, but that did not matter. We never had a problem getting what we wanted. It was not a problem

to ask anyone in their early adult y
buy alcohol for us and 99 percent would
without hesitation. After that was completed, ou
supernatural powers would take place.

Some of our gatherings were furnished with at least one keg, if not more. Getting in trouble was part of the action. There were always a couple of guys who loved to show up, without notice or permission. It was obvious that they were not a part of our crowd. They always seemed to show off the great accomplishments of their drinking over a period of time, which caused problems. That led to our resultant behavior.

By the end, it did not matter in any case; the fight was on. The guys and I would jump right into it, in partnership with that fizzy stuff that was influencing our attitudes. We would always scrape with some unknown mates along the way. There was never a concern about it because we all were close by. Around the same time that this would take place, we would get the company of another group of unwanted friends. The law would always pop in unexpectedly to ruin the bash.

ge of people try alcohol, drugs, ...ctivities that impair their well-...ecomes a problem, that's when ...rboard. My friends and I would ... this happen to people at the pa... , in most cases, it involved the first one in that list, alcohol. Alcohol was a big part of my family. For as long as I could remember, the drinking game was for real. This was a common involvement. It also must have been in our blood or something like that.

My family's friends were just like the ones that I picked up—consumers. All the family, relatives, and friends would do their own thing, but together. Before, during, and after I was born, all these people loved to socialize and drink. When growing up as a young child to an early teen, I simply watched and learned from afar. It was very comfortable being around them, and it looks like that's where I picked up my problem. I may as well point the finger at myself, because it was I who repeatedly picked up the bottle or can of alcohol.

Saturday's were exciting! Normally, we would hit Clearwater or Maderia beach. High schools had their own hot spots, or hanging places. During the day, it was always a rowdy, fun event, if you know what I mean. There was volleyball, skim-boarding, paddle ball, surfing (if the waves were ever up), and different people doing different things. Maderia beach was the place to slam the brews down.

One weekend, I saw one of my best friends sitting a few feet away, free from stress, next to a priceless, cold six-pack of beer. So I yelled to Joe, "Hey, man, send me one of those stressful, cold cans." As he tossed it over in my direction, I went up for the catch, but because of the ice water on the can, it slipped right through my hands and hit me in the face, causing one of my eyes to swell.

He and I became best friends when I was eight years old. We loved to be outside, fishing, playing, riding our bikes, building tree forts, and just having fun. He lived just around the corner from me and his parents were cool too. They became good friends with my mom and dad. As of now, I can still call him my best friend.

After leaving the beach, I would venture home to grab dinner (either McDonald's or Mom's). I had to take a shower and try to be a notably good-looking young mate. Then, I had to make a round of phone calls. After making contact, it was time to hit the town. My plans always included a large crowd of people.

We would meet at a chosen destination, and then proceed on to our adventures. A large percentage of the people there would already have beer or liquor with us. I was always prepared.

Me, my Plymouth Valiant, and a twelve pack of beer

It got some of the crowd in a better mood before we would head out into the town or to a party.

Chapter 3
Relationships

During my late teens and early twenties, I undertook all kinds of different relationships. They all had their own issues and affected my life in different ways. It was obvious that a couple of them would take a little bit more of my time and effort than others. No matter what, it seemed that girls were always in the picture. Hooking up with young ladies seemed to be a regular procedure for me. Naturally, each woman had a different outlook on life. I very much enjoyed the moments I spent with some of them. With the other young ladies, there was apparently a problem, and it had to do with their attitudes toward religion.

Church had become an issue within a couple of my relationships. It seemed that it was on a few girlfriends' minds, though it was not on my mind. We could never see eye to eye on this topic. For me, it just did not make sense. Why should I have to strain my eyes? They had their family-style life. I guess at some age they had found their calling. At that time, I was just not receiving any calls. I was just doubtful about sitting down to hear any words from their mouths that would direct my life and or tell me how it should be lived.

God, Jesus, the place where He lived, and the church that represented Him were not important in my life at the time. There was something unclear about the whole situation. I must have had questions somewhere inside my brain, but I didn't focus on them. I was concerned with myself, not Him! I had been told about how things happen in other peoples' lives that made them see the big picture and how their lives have changed, but it was not a concern in my life. It seemed dim to me to focus on worshiping and the supposed good it brought people.

My eyes were not set on this mental image and I had no plans regarding it for the future. Looking back, I guess it was because I did not want to give up my time or space. I did not want to see what came from devotion. As for my family, they were living their own lives. Yes, we all were still united as a family, but we were caught up in the day-by-day routines. There must have been some indication that my family assumed that God was still present in their lives, but that moment in our cycle was not in sync with His cycle. I only focused on Him (for a short time) when something major happened in my life.

There was another source of joy in my life. It was children. I very much enjoyed being around them. I had my younger cousins, family, and friends who had their own, and some of them lived in the neighborhood. It was fun being active with them. The only reason I say this was because I loved being that way. We would do everything from coloring with crayons to swimming in the pool, riding bikes, and eating ice cream.

Little kids are free to be themselves. It seems like the only care they have in this world is to have fun and enjoy what life has to offer, and that's how it should be. They shouldn't have to worry about anything at all. I prefer children from the ages of one day to about seven or eight years old. That was my strongest point, and after that it s-l-o-w-l-y goes down.

Something that did take more of my time and space was the job thing. Jobs were easy to come by. At my age, if you got tired of one job you could just move onto the next. I went through a lot of jobs in that time. When I was nineteen, I got a job at a surf shop. I loved the beach, surfing, skim-boarding and cool clothes. My friends would always come in to check out the place and hang out. I also met some new friends. Life was great.

For one thing, beach activities were always intense. Surfing was a favorite activity of mine. My best friends, other guys, and I would gather up to ride the waves or go to the other coast swells. We always had to go where the waves were up. When the tropical storms or hurricanes (from a distance) started moving towards the east or west of the state they would bring some very nice swells.

Most of our cars had these racks attached to the top of them that allowed us to strap down our surfboards. The guys and I would have a blast on these trips, and we did some crazy things along the way. During this one trip, three of my friends and I exited from Interstate 4 to take a two-lane road to the East Coast, heading for Sebastian Inlet. As I drove my car, we noticed a lot of trees, grass, long fences, fields, and cows. So, after pulling over to the side of the road, Daniel and I ran to the fence, made our way through it, and started chasing these cows everywhere! After arriving at our final destination, it was time to get wet.

Lifting weights is good for the body, and I loved it. My other best friend, Paul, and I would continually pump iron. The two of us hit it off and became good friends when I started dating his sister, Tracy. His parents slowly became like surrogate parents, and that continued even after his sister and I split up. To this day, I can still call him my best friend.

Paul and I, furthermore, liked getting fit because it attracted the ladies! Football, now that's a sport. Man, a few of the guys and I would watch our favorite team every week. Back in those days, I liked San Francisco '49ers. There were times when we all would get together on this field and play for hours. At the end of the game, we would huddle around to chat and talk about our wounds.

My parents were pretty cool about giving me freedom because they trusted me. They gave me encouragement to do almost anything I set my mind too. Emotionally, I was at peace and found myself to be physically and mentally quick. Because of this, it had come naturally to me to be interested in several different sports and ways of life. As for the ways of life, there was one in particular that started when I was a child and stuck with me up to this point.

Many people I knew, including myself, drank alcohol for many reasons. I had seen real photos before I was born that involved family members and the presence of alcohol. As for growing up, it was eternally a part of life. Drinking alcohol was a part of almost everything: daily life at home, parties, and honoring sports. It was performed at our dwelling, especially when we had huge gatherings with family and friends. And, this absorbing of alcohol took place outside of our home.

Beer was a part of stockcar racing. I must have been around seven years old when my family and our friends went to the Daytona International Speedway. There was a camping area inside the track. It would only accommodate a certain amount of people because of the space, but our van made it in. My parents and their friends had the supplies: camping equipment, food, water, and beer. We had beer everywhere. In those days, it seemed like partying lasted forever.

The racetrack back home where I grew up was no different. Alcohol was not allowed in the pits (the area where the pit crews worked on the cars) during the races.

That's why families and friends would bring portable coolers with bottles and cans of that beer. Once we left the track the only thing in the portable coolers was cold water.

Finally, I got the opportunity to join the family history book in 1991. Steve and I decided to find a race car for me. We searched around for a mini-stock—a small four-cylinder vehicle. A short time later, and we found this guy who was selling his mini-stock. After making repairs, I was beating and banging for a position on the racetrack. The number ten was painted on the side of my car as I went by the audience and fans.

My race car and I

Chapter 4
Turning Point in Life

By now, the age of twenty-one was just around the bend. Life was looking better and better for me because of the opportunities this would bring. I would have the right to act like a real adult. That was a big step. Surely, it was more than just a night of racing cars, venturing out at nights, hanging with friends, getting into trouble, dating younger girls, and working. Now I could *buy* alcohol and go to real clubs. This meant no more asking, tipping, or giving away some our cheap beer in the process of acquiring it.

If only I could have been wiser and foreseen what would come into existence. My father and I had already been working off and on together for many years. We loved the satisfaction of working outside. I really didn't like to be inside. The good thing about it was that we were always engaged in an activity. This was a job where you could be your own boss, in a way. My dad was something like a contractor, and he had a license that involved the installation of windows, screen porches, and coolroofs.

My father was very knowledgeable regarding developing aluminum structures. All I can say is that he could do just about any trade. Before asphalt paving, my dad had done a lot of home remodeling. He was good, smart with all hand and electric tools, and he wasn't afraid of getting his hands dirty.

Jeff and I had learned a lot from hands-on training. My dad, brother, and I sometimes worked together, like the three musketeers. Dad was a partner in a business that got us the jobs, and we'd do the installation. We liked working together and the money we made.

It was Friday, August 23, 1991. Just a few days had passed since my birthday. My dad was hired to install a coolroof for a customer. This coolroof was different compared to what you normally saw around town. It was a panel made from aluminum that had been glued to a kind of foam that was a few inches thick. We'd occasionally installed them on mobile homes and houses that had flat roofs. The flat roofs were like additions that were added on from the main house.

Dad and I had shown up to this one; I don't remember where Jeff was. We had our own little tasks to get the job done quickly. I would unload everything, get it all set up, and Dad would take care of any problems with the roof before installing those panels, like fixing rotted wood and so on.

This house had tile, but we were doing the flat roof section, so the tile had to be removed in order to cut down to the existing wood. The panels had to slide under the roofing material, and then we'd have to caulk between the two layers with a roofing sealer. This customer's house took most of the day. As we were finishing up, I went ahead and started gathering up the leftover tools and cleaning up the area. Some of the tile had to come down because the panels took over the space.

So, I would take five or six tiles down the ladder. This time, however, I lost my balance. It all happened so fast. I let go of the tiles, trying to soften the fall and not hurt myself. I hit the ground with a *bang*. It did not feel good.

After being dazed, I was able to pick myself up. My hand moved straight to my head. Wow. I looked around to find the customer's hose. Once I found it I felt relief. The cold water cooled the throbbing. I just sat there because of the pain. Soon after this had taken place, my father approached, and saw me with the hose to my head. "We're almost done. What happened?" he asked. "I fell off the ladder and hit my head," I replied. A couple minutes later, I got the rest of the tile off the roof and then it was time to go.

The hours that had led up to Friday evening were gone, and all of a sudden it was upon me. Regan, the young lady I was dating at the time, had come over to my mother's house. My entire life up to that point had been spent living there. Soon the phone started ringing off the hook. It was the normal crowd wanting to go out. I could not overlook my head still hurting at this point. It was a common feeling, so I had just assumed that it was a bad headache. After speaking to a few people, it was apparent that I did not feel like going out and wanted to stay home for the night.

A new day had arrived—August the twenty-fourth. It was a Saturday morning, and it sure was beautiful outside. I had plans for that morning. Regan's parents had bought another house down the street from where they had been living and they needed a hand moving. When I arrived at the house, they put me to work. We packed all the little stuff up in our trucks and cars, which took a few trips. After that I helped move some bigger stuff, like furniture, bedroom items, and so on.

Her dad, Rodger, and I had one major thing in common: he had owned a race car around my age. I had seen a picture of his car. He had the opportunity to be present at couple of my races.

By this time, I found myself taking aspirin because the headache was getting worse. I just couldn't see myself going to the doctor for a bad headache. That's how I felt about the whole situation.

A couple of my friends were with me to help move Regan's family into their new house. They were the same friends who had tried to talk me into going out with them the night before.

As the day proceeded, I was presented with the idea of going to a party later that night. Inside, the only thing I had planned for later that night was being at home and going to sleep! Knowing that I had not gone out the night before, their peer-pressure got to me, and they won. You could tell by seeing their faces that this victory pleased them.

A guy dealing with this much peer-pressure when hanging with his pals has a hard time saying no. Hey, a night out with the fellows and aspirin on the side sounded all right. I left Regan's house and went back home. Late in the afternoon, I spoke to one of my friends on the phone about going out with him. My head was now pounding, but I overlooked it to hang out with my friends for the night. So, I got ready and went over to his house. I only remember small bits of my actions after this point.

As if they were flashbacks, I remember being at that party for a second (but not where it was), people being around me at times (but not who they were), and then being at an old hang-out spot, and getting out of Regan's car. That was it.

Sunday morning was here—the twenty-fifth of August. As I tried to recall the previous night, my friend told me about the night: how I had drank some alcohol, and how I had passed out in his car. He also mentioned a lot of people who had shown up at the places we went. For sure, it was sleep that I had needed, and wanted! I could recall this. So, I eventually stormed home to my waterbed. It must have been around noon, maybe later. When I arrived home, I slept, slept, and continued to sleep. I cannot remember if my mom came into my room, though she probably did.

It was Monday the twenty-sixth of August. I was in the same condition then as I had been the previous afternoon. My entire body was completely at ease because of my waterbed. I don't remember if I even thought of seeing a doctor about my headache at this moment. From this point, I can only try to explain my condition based on information from my loved ones.

Mom came into my room around eight o'clock and said that Joe (my best friend) was here. He would sometimes make extra money working with my dad and me. As he entered my room, it looked like I was still half asleep. Trying to get my attention, he received little feedback. So, he even tried to lightly push me to get a better reaction. I could barely mumble in response.

The tone of my voice echoing out made me sound highly intoxicated. He must have realized something might be wrong. He would normally know if I had done something out of the ordinary. As he exited my bedroom, my mother spoke to him. He was concerned about my well-being. As for leaving the house, he just told my mom about working with my dad and that he would call me later in the day.

It probably would have been good for me to tell my mother to stay home and not go to work. I did not say much to her. Normally, we talked all the time. "I am leaving for work," she finally told me. She must have been a little worried. I was her baby, after all.

Before leaving, she made a phone call to her boyfriend, Steve, and told him about the way I was acting. She did not feel comfortable leaving me at home. He did not live far away, and he said that he'd stop by and check on me. I must have been falling in and out of sleep; the clock was completely out of sight, but ticking.

My mother left for work somewhere between eight and eight-thirty. I only wish that I had been able to stop her before she left. Why couldn't I just have asked her to take me to the doctor? If I had gotten her take me, the following probably would not have happened. Still, if anyone had spoken to me, I don't even know if I could have responded.

I was told later that Steve had swung by the house to check on me. I do not even remember him saying "Hello." After leaving the house, he spoke to my mom at work and told her that I seemed to be all right. From that point on, the only movement my body made was the beating of my heart. Everything else, including my mind, had shut down.

My mom arrived back home around one-thirty or two. By then, my sluggish state of mind had become more profound. She entered my room, trying to get my attention. When I did not respond, she quickly dialed nine-one-one and explained my condition to the operator. It only took a couple of minutes for the fire truck and ambulance to arrive at our house. They went straight into my room with the seconds ticking. Looking back, my mother must have thought they were angels who had come to my rescue.

The paramedics and emergency medical technicians (EMT's) had to assess the nature of my condition and quickly investigate whether I had any pre-existing medical conditions that might have contributed to my current condition. Firefighters were present to give a hand if they were needed. As the paramedics and EMT's continued their mission, it became apparent that they would not find any physical indication regarding the cause of my injury. I had no cuts, scratches, bruises, or marks of any kind anywhere on my body! Obviously, it had been falling off the ladder and hitting my head on the ground that had caused my condition, but I could not explain this. When they couldn't find anything during their examination, I was rushed to the emergency room. Thank goodness there was a hospital only two or three miles from my house. That turned out to be important because I did not have much more time.

One of the doctors on duty at the emergency room was a gentleman named Jeffery. He was a brain surgeon. I had to undergo a well-performed examination of my head to see what might be the cause of this trauma. After the study, he announced to my mother that I had a physical injury between my skull and brain. This head injury had caused an enormous blood clot that had entered the left side of my head. My skull had to be opened so that the blood clot could be removed.

Jeffery informed my mother that I had sustained a subdural hematoma (SDH). It was a traumatic brain injury in which blood gathers between the dura (the outer protective covering of the brain) and the arachoid (the middle layer of the meninges). The dura mater, arachnoid mater, and the pita mater protect the central nervous system.

The procedure needed to be done promptly. The doctor told my mother about the procedure and the risks before moving forward with this surgery. He also told her that if she had come home an hour or so later I most likely wouldn't have been alive. Without hesitation, he got the approval to perform the procedure from my mother. The doctor was prepared, set, and ready to operate. He opened up my skull in order to drain the blood. The very long incision was shaped just like a question mark. It was spooky.

The mind is crucial to everything we undertake in life. A great percentage of people strive to use as much of their minds as they can. I have been told we only use a small portion of our brains, and are still able to excel.

I found out that the left sides of our brains process speech, analysis, time, and sequence. It can recognize letters, numbers, and words. The right sides of our brains process creativity, patterns, spatial awareness, and context. It can recognize faces, places, and objects. The two sides of our brain are called hemispheres. They both have independent functions. My injury was on my left side.

By this time, I must have been fully in someone else's hands because my hands were not moving and I could not feel a thing! I could not hear, see, speak, walk, or use any other part of my body.

My head had been shaved where the incision had been made. I guess the hospital was more focused on my operation than my looks! After the surgery was completed, I laid in a coma. A good percentage of my family and friends were in the lobby comforting one another, crying, waiting, walking, and praying. My condition was going to increase everyone's emotional stress, upsetting hearts and perplexing minds. As a result of the subdural hematoma, a major problem emerged.

Later that night, with blood on the brain, it had started to swell, so a second surgery had to be performed. Jeffery had to reduce the swelling, reopening the question mark just behind my ear and removing a small portion of the temporal bone. This solved the problem and controlled the swelling.

For days ahead my condition looked very uncertain. The hospital filled with people who cared for and loved me. My family and friends were still comforting one another, crying, waiting, walking, and praying. I lay in a coma for a week, and then another week went by. I showed no visible signs of recovery. I was still in the state of no-mind! I could not even imagine what Harold and Jenny were going through or thinking during these days, not to mention the other members of my family and friends.

During that time, the doctor and nurses gave their sympathy to all, especially my mom. If my knowledge is correct, she had replied to them by asking them to not touch me or remove anything from me. She believed in my recovery, and in me. She wanted my heart, mind, soul, and strength to be strong. It's a good thing she felt this way. My mother and everyone else must have spoken to the Lord a lot, even when they left the hospital. Their prayers had to have been growing stronger and stronger each day. It must have been this Lord that improved my well-being and state of mind.

After two and a half weeks, I was able to come out of the coma. Eventually, the nurses had moved me from the emergency room into a hospital room. I stayed there for a couple more weeks.

To think that I was someone who loved the world, riding bikes, roller skating for hours at a time, playing football, surfing, weightlifting, stockcar racing, and so much more, and now I could not do one thing. I could not even adjust a small portion of my body!

Chapter 5

Recovery

The next obstacle in my life was something that I had not foreseen. Someone had a big future planned for me that neither my family, nor I knew about. My mother had enrolled me into HealthSouth Rehabilitation Center, hoping to aid my recovery process. It was the kind of encouragement that everyone around me was hoping for. A pleasing older gentleman who was employed by this center arrived at the hospital. The van he drove had a lift for wheelchairs. That is how I was transported to the rehabilitation center located in Largo, Florida.

HealthSouth was an institute where, if I were to surmount my injury, the strength would have to come from within me. This older gentleman had the generosity to transport my mother and me. My ability was very limited. As we took the trip to the center, I remembered a small portion of it as I gazed out of the window, watching vehicles passing us by.

I could only see out of my right eye because of the surgery. My left eye had shut completely. The visible part surrounding the bone-line cavity had moved all the way to my left side, closing the eye lid. Later in my recovery, the thin fold of skin that covered my eye slowly opened, though my eyeball took much longer to return to its normal position.

Arriving and entering this center by wheelchair, I had no clue where I was. It was as if my body was the only thing entering this building. Imagine being in this condition, wherein it seems that your mind is unplugged from your body, and imagine learning how to drink from a cup, pick up a fork or pencil, sleep properly in a bed (without hurting yourself), speak, walk, and even take a shower all over again. That was my future.

Being inside the rehab center, all kinds of people were already living there. I did not know what was wrong with them. I noticed a few who were around my age, but a larger percentage of the residents were from the older generation.

The staff members were involved with the patients, to help them achieve their goals. They would go overboard, making sure that their duties were performed following the proper procedures, and that it was safe for the individuals trying to achieve recovery. This place was completely conducive to my recovery, and the staff made absolutely sure that all their treatments were conducted properly. HealthSouth had the latest exercise equipment, computers to improve speech, housing supplies to enhance the individual's well-being, and so much more.

I was a baby for the second time. I had to learn how to do everything all over again. For about a month in their small cafeteria, I remember being fed in a wheelchair, but I cannot remember who fed me. As my mind started helping my body, I was able to learn how to walk again with an assistant. Initially, I used two bars on either side of me for support and balance as I tried to take my first steps. Another time, I used a white rope to pull up and down on a small, thin square, which I now know was a weight machine.

The center encouraged me to improve. There was a young woman who worked with patients on the activity of speech and movement. Her name was Tina. She assisted patients with improving their sounds, actions, reactions, and their ability to think of how to physically respond. During one of my first classes, Tina worked on my reactions and coordination by using items and the following of hand movements.

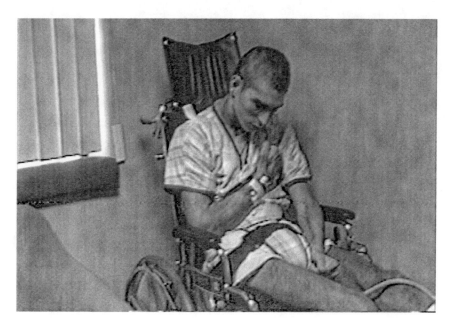

I had just entered Tina's classroom for a lesson

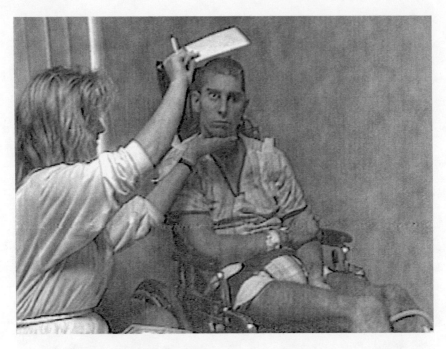

*I was told to follow her hand movement with my
eye and try to keep my head from moving*

She wanted me to reply the answer to her, even if I could not speak

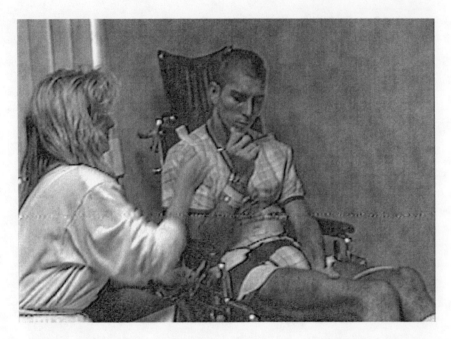

She wanted me to respond to her, in the proper
way of holding onto and using a pencil to write

I remember another visit to her room when I sat in front of a computer. I had to adjust my speech to the action of sound waves. While hearing these waves, I had to increase and decrease my vocal chords. As I paid attention and responded to the sound waves my voice emerged slowly. This improved my communication. The rehabilitation center had different classes at different times during my residence there.

With extraordinary hard work and dedication I was able to complete the goals that were set before me, improving my well-being. Using a fork and spoon became more manageable. I even began to take my first steps on my own. A female nurse had an enormous heart and really helped me to improve my ability to walk. She would sometimes stop my wheelchair just a few of feet from my room, walk a couple of steps in front of me, and then say, "If you walk to me, I'll push you the rest of the way." I got mad because I did not want to walk. It was fun sitting in the wheelchair and being pushed around. It felt like I was moving fast again, like being in a car.

Eventually she won, and I would walk the couple of steps, and then she would push me to my room (which felt like my home). It was where I would either sleep or watch television. With everyone's assistance my walking improved. During my experience at the center, I met a very cool young guy and his wife who worked there. Our relationship became stronger because we started finding out about each other. He told me some things about his life, and I told him some things about mine. One thing that I found out was that his cousin was one of the guys I had hung out and surfed with before my accident.

The members of the rehabilitation center must have seen that I was making progress; I was allowed to go outside. We would travel on the sidewalk around the whole building. It was such a relief because it felt really good to be outside again. I was able to learn about friendships again too. I did not really remember the meaning of friendship. I had to get a grip on that all over again. My new friend went out of his way to show me kindness.

It was a series of events that restored my qualities. Comprehending these different emotions and gaining the ability to adjust to them only added to my improvement. My emotions had to overcome my body, as though the reconstruction of my knowledge had not affected my feelings. I had to learn to express what I felt inside—to give and receive. My language, at times, seemed to affect my behavior in the eyes of some of the staff members, before I got a reasonable handle on it. Still, there was a part of me that did not know how to respond.

I guess it was because of the way that they did their job at that time. I did not allow them to do certain operations, but only because I did not like those certain operations. At the time, I was a child who just did not know how to react. I wish now that I could simply say sorry to those people.

Being able to speak, move my arms, hands, legs, and feet, chew up food and swallow it, drink water, and regain the ability to adjust to life made it more suitable for me.

There are some things that I cannot describe during my time at the center, like relearning to use a pencil. I just do not remember. I am extremely sure, though, that the staff members went out of their way to improve my well-being!

The number of visitors I received was on the rise and pleasing to me. With only slight difficulty, I could even respond to others. My entire family would stop in to bug me—just kidding. I loved their company, and they were happy to see my improvements.

Some of my friends had even visited the rehabilitation center. As a matter of fact, one of my little cousins would arrive at the center with his family carrying a canvas tote. It was filled up with all sorts of different objects and toys that he brought from his bedroom. He would reach into this canvas tote and show one of these objects and toys to me. Then he would ask, "Do you know what this is?" I had to trick him by saying no so that he would explain everything to me. I wanted to make him feel like a big man. When they first started visiting me, I was told that his mother had told him that I had to learn everything again, so that must have been why the little guy acted out his part.

On another occasion, my best friend, Paul, brought one of my favorite movies with him. It was a movie that had to do with stockcar racing called *Days of Thunder*, and I loved that. We would sit for hours at a time watching this movie. It was like we were brothers. Paul and I had watched a lot of other movies before my accident.

One visit was exceptionally exciting because my mom told me to come outside with her. She and her boyfriend, Steve, had brought Fritz, my doggy, up to the center for me. I very much loved having my buddy lick me to death all over. It was refreshing to have the presence of my family, friends, and my dog. The series of visits by my loved ones started a sensitivity reaction. I began to experience a strong love for them that I had not felt since my ordeal.

Chapter 6
Having a Desire

Day by day, week by week, and month by month, the time added up. I felt as if I would never leave this place, as if the center was now my home. Finally I received some good news. It was said that I would be going home, and the day was marked on the calendar. This was the information I needed to survive. Living in the hospital and the center for a little over four months, I had almost forgotten about having a real home. It was like I was going to another new place, only my family would be there.

I sure did miss my home. A person can't ever really know how much they miss their home until they are away from it for a good period of time. Take it from someone who personally went through trauma and time away from home. It was sincerely on my mind. When the opportunity had come to me, it seemed to put the world in the palm of my hands.

Finally, it was the day I was to go home, to the place where I had developed from a newborn into a twenty-one-year-old man. My family came to the center to pick me up. Arriving at home was so refreshing. I hadn't seen my driveway or house in months. Walking into my front door felt unnatural. There was something different about it all because I was so used to the center, you know. Being inside, I found much comfort. It felt as if my body, mind, and soul would not let go of my family's spirit and my wonderful dog's love.

I felt at peace, a peace that made a warm, smooth feeling flow through my blood from my head down to my toes. I had the time to relish these moments. Being around my family and having their touch was so important. It was a source of love that a person needs and families need this as much as the other person. My family had experienced major comfort in their souls upon my return.

I would not be home long because a time limit had been set upon it. As I recall, I thought I was home for good, but I was not. Mom told me that I was only given the opportunity to go home for a short time. I guess it was to see how I would react. I didn't put two and two together to realize that I was just going home for the day. So, the drive back to the HealthSouth upset me a great deal. When I arrived back at the center, I entered my room and quickly lay in my bed, thinking of home. I felt sad and lonely. It appeared that I would never get out.

Using my partially repaired brain, I thought about home, my family, and Fritz. I thought about how much we had shared together. It became obvious that I wanted to go back home right then! "But," I thought, "How can I if Mom already left and this place won't let me walk out the front door?" That's when I got an idea. The nurse had just come into my room to check on me and do her duty. When she had left, I instigated my plan to escape!

There was no turning back. I tried to put on some clothes that would not stand out. I remember putting on a surfer's knitted pullover with a hood. I did this thinking that no one would see me, as if I were a normal human being walking down the street. I don't remember what else I put on.

First, I was able to get the window unlocked and opened. Second, I was able to exit through the window and shut it, but it somehow locked itself when it shut, or at least that's what they said. My next move was to cross the lawn and get to the sidewalk. I was a free man! I felt like I had just escaped from prison—climbing the wall, jumping in the water, and swimming to the other side.

Remember my friend whom I had walked with around the center? That is exactly what I did—remember my walks outside in order to finish making my escape. I knew my way around a little, and I had seen certain landmarks. The sidewalk was a short distance from the main road, and then taking a right turn on the sidewalk (walking in front of the center) would bring me to a stop light, and to the right was a gas station.

At this point, I made it to where I had seen a pay phone. I remembered that if you press zero, you could reach the operator. After getting her on the other end, I asked her to place a call to my parents. I do not remember if I told the operator a number or my mother's full name. I do remember that she told my mom that she had a collect call. "Hello," my mother said. "Come and get me," I told her. "What?" she said, expressing disbelief.

She did not understand. "Where are you?" she asked. I told her that I was at a gas station next to the center, and to come and get me.

She could not believe that her son was *there*. My sister quickly used another phone to call them. She asked if I was in my room. They checked, and replied that, no, I wasn't. The word got out, and officers, a fire truck, an ambulance, and the young lady who was in charge of HealthSouth that evening showed up.

I am sure if you were to look around at the scene, you'd have thought that someone had been injured or even killed. I am guessing the cops wanted to take me to jail. The young lady just wanted to take me to the center where I was living forever, it seemed. My mother and others very soon showed up as the officers were surrounding the exit doors.

I suppose that after my escape attempt, the management at the rehabilitation center got the message that I was ready to go home. It did not take long after that ordeal. I learned that I would soon return to my real home again. It only took about two more weeks before I received my departing papers. I just needed and wanted to go home to be with my family, friends, and dog. It was so satisfying to know that I was going back to the place where the people who loved me would surround me.

Very soon after leaving the rehabilitation center as an inpatient, I became an outpatient. Outpatients received the same treatment as others at the center, depending on which health problem they were dealing with at the time. I had to be picked up and then brought home during the week. I did not have to go to HealthSouth on the weekends. The cool thing about it, I got the pleasing older gentleman who picked up my mom and me from the hospital.

He always showed up at our house at the same time when I became an outpatient. During my journeys to the center, I noticed other young people with different conditions. They all had their own personally uncontrollable actions. I had even seen one person use a microphone that he held up against his throat in order to speak. That was a very depressing sight for me. I felt sorry for him. I always tried to be a friend to those patients. They were all like me. We all needed some type of treatment in order to succeed. We were people who stood out from the crowd—helpless but determined souls who were bound to complete our destiny.

I was just getting tired with the treatment, equipment, rehabilitation center, and myself. The people there seemed to need more than I did at the time. Being a part of the outpatient procedure soon bored me, and I wanted to move forward. I found that in order for me to improve, I would have to step up to the plate, so I told my mother about it. Soon, my mother decided to help me spread my wings. She enrolled me at another rehabilitation center. I thought it was the appropriate thing to do. I don't remember if any patients lived there. I think it was just a place for outpatients. When I got there and started the program, I could not believe their process of teaching. Unquestionably, this education did not do a thing for me. This place was not for me! I wished that I had never left the old rehab center where I once lived.

Chapter 7
Faith

Meanwhile, as I took two steps forward to repair my life, it seemed that I also took a step back. I was determined to move forward again and again. I knew that there had to be a reason for my attitude and determination. When I thought back on the accident and what had led up to this point in my life, it seemed that there must have been another person next to me. It was completely obvious that this other person had to have been very strong because I was not.

I realized that all of those prayers from both sides of my family and friends that were offered both silently and aloud had apparently worked. God absolutely must have been working in my life.

When people told me about all the prayers that went out for me, I was overwhelmed by the simple fact that I was alive! This made me think, how could God be a part of my life when I was so far from being a part of His?

The next stage of my life would soon be rearranged. If He was so prevalent in my life, why would He put me through this pain all over again? In December 1993, I had started occasionally helping my father do some side jobs. My father was doing the same type of work. One Friday evening, we spoke on the phone about a job he had to do on this mobile home. He asked whether I could give him a hand with this job and gave me directions. I said, sure, it's no problem. We would normally just say goodbye and that would be it, but at that instance, he replied, "I love you."

Wow, I did not see that coming! It made me feel uncomfortable for a moment because that wasn't like him. It was Saturday morning, and I was getting ready to go work with my dad. All of a sudden, I changed my mind and did not go. That was unusual for me. The day passed, and I got a call that evening. A member of my step-mom's family informed me bluntly that my dad had died from a heart attack at a job he had been doing that day. Hanging up the phone, I dropped to my knees. I cried unbearably. The thought of being there, that I could have saved his life, haunted me. Why had I chosen not to go?

No one was present at my home, and I promptly called Jeff. I think a friend drove me over to my brother's house. Jeff, Sandy, and I cried together. That was it, the end to my relationship with my father. He was only fifty-four years of age. Our families were emotional, but a couple of us were destroyed. It was my dad. I just wished we had been closer then we were, like my mom and I. His death left an empty spot in my heart that will never be filled.

Adding to this, I had another terrifying event that took a toll on me. This other tragedy involved another deep love that filled my whole heart. My rottweiler had become ill. Fritz had been feeling this way for a few days. So, my mother and I decided he needed to go to the animal hospital. The visit was not easy for me. The veterinarian said that my dog had an autoimmune disease. He announced that the best thing we could do was to put him to sleep. It was very difficult for me to leave, knowing that I was never going to be able to play with him again. I very much cherish the time we spent together. My dog was gone.

With these two important parts of my life gone, I needed a major restoration to take place.

If God was so much a part of my life, how could He do this to me? I did not understand. I simply could not believe that this had happened, but I had to try. I needed some source of comfort. The internal parts of my body could not deal with the reality of the situation.

What could His plan for me be, when it called for my loved ones to leave my life? It must be similarly difficult for other people who have to go through similar trials. They probably have to dwell on this mystery for some time.

It's a shift in people's lives that cannot be controlled. I had to examine what it meant to me.

My question was: why do tragedies have to happen when people are not ready for them? In everyone's life, they seem to come without notice. I needed whatever God could offer me to restore my prosperous state of being. With time I slowly started to understand the meaning of life.

I realized that nobody is perfect. I unquestionably realized that only God was. I saw my spiritual existence as a building block in constructing a meaning for my life. This construction also involved who I was as a person. It was obvious that the future of my life was already outlined. I just did not see the outline.

My process of development continued in a positive direction. I felt stronger about my life and who I was. I noticed that some people moved on with their lives without even caring about themselves or others around them. It is always better to be proud of yourself than to be an unknown. The way you act may be predicated on what you think that people see you as.

There might be a person somewhere out in this crazy, wonderful world who might be looking for or needing to find you. Or, it could even be the other way around. For some god-forsaken reason, this might be to show affection or some kind of support. Everyone has a purpose in life.

If you are alive here on earth, there is a reason for it. Moving on with my life was part of the process, but finding my destiny meant more. With time, starting something new would be the only way for me to take control. As I took two more steps, I did not step back. In fact, I gained the ability to walk faster. Maybe getting stronger was a part of reaching adulthood. After this kind of tragedy, I realized that my strength was vital. My family was taking steps toward potentially being in control of their own destinies at the same speed I was.

During those years, my family had decided to refresh their religions. It had been an obvious move for my brother to switch. He got married at a Baptist church. Sandy, his wife, already belonged to that church. At this point in Lisa's life, she had met a new man who was a Christian at another church. His name was Greg. They quickly developed a close relationship. They hit it off, and the next thing you know there were wedding bells ringing. He was and is very true to her. To this day, their marriage is still about being faithful. It is very satisfying to find that one person to spend the rest of your life with. This effective force absorbs your whole eternal self. Her husband highly respects the Lord.

Mom soon devoted herself to another church. It was the First Baptist Church of Indian Rocks located in Largo, Florida. She loved their church services, the people, and the evening events. The

Catholic life was nowhere to be found in my life, and was no longer doing anything for me by this time.

Like I said, we all just drifted away from Catholicism. My mom asked me if I wanted to go with her to church. For me, that was a big leap because leading up to my accident, I had wanted nothing to do with that.

She informed me that the pastor simply spoke the truth about life at her church and that the words were not copied, nor were they from a book. She told me that when Pastor Charlie talked or preached, the words just flowed from his heart, soul, and mind. He talked of his and other people's experiences, which blended into the words of the Bible. I went with her to one of his services. I couldn't believe what I just heard. He made me feel so much at home. The services had helped me realize more and more about the common difference between Jesus and God. I learned more about the meaning of life.

It showed me also that you do not always have to go into a church and kneel down for hours at a given time to be in touch with God. I realized that I could talk to him whenever and wherever I was in life. I felt blessed in life, and I found energy from speaking to Him when stopping at a traffic light. I had to learn more. My powers of observation were getting stronger. Being a part of this new church required my mother and I to renew our vows. That's when we gave our whole revived souls and spirits to the Lord. We both were transformed, purified in His water. I received a strong feeling of affection. It spread over my entire body.

My mom had some friends and met new ones while going to this church. She had spoken to one of the pastors about my accident and testimony. His name was Pastor Gary. When I meet him, he was just like me—filled with energy and full of life. He and I became very close friends; it was as if someone had already planned it. As I got more involved with this church, I also volunteered in the children's program.

This had increased my desire to work with children. The time I spent with kids learning about Jesus helped me to learn more about whom He was, and that maybe that was where I should be. The stories about Jesus and the pastor's experiences rang so true. Starting my new Christian formation, I started to think about the future.

Back in high school, I had no desire to participate in this kind of formal religious setting. All that I desired was to do my own thing, but now all that I desired was this new growth. It was pretty cool, and I loved working with kids! I began thinking about the future and what I should do with mine. There must have been someone knocking on my door, trying to get my attention, but I couldn't hear it. I just moved forward until I saw the door.

Chapter 8
Education

A great, outstanding thought arose in my mind, as if someone had spoken it to me. I was ready for the challenge because of my past experiences and education. Having these two very important parts in my life allowed me to make the right decision. I announced to my mother that I wanted to go to college and improve my education. She happily agreed.

My skills, reaction, and other personal accomplishments were set for learning. Basically, before this time I had been a zombie. I had become a normal human being. So, I decided that taking the appropriate action would be the right path. I had started driving again after taking a major review of my abilities behind the stirring wheel. So, with transportation, I was able to extend a large helping hand to myself.

I went to St. Petersburg Junior College to enroll. Again, I had to take the pretest. I thought that there was no need for studying. I assumed it was going to be breeze. It was *not*. Boy did that turn out bad, just as it had before. A higher power must have been in control because I stayed this time. They put me in every basic class. As it turned out, I guess my mind was still around that level. Those classes were sure for beginners. They involved basic writing, basic reading, and basic math!

I started my classes in January 1994. My communication skills were more than suitable for school. This helped me to be forceful and move forward. I got a wonderful teacher who was an English instructor. Her name was Evelyn. She had pointed me in the right direction, helping me to understand the concepts by taking the time to explain them. She helped me increase my ability to put words to paper. She was so generous to me, as if she knew of my past.

The other classes were valuable too. I found myself learning more. I thought that more education would make me a better, smarter person.

I started interacting with other students. We would talk about school, work, and our personal lives. Sometimes God was an important topic.

We all had questions about Him, and we helped each other understand. I increased my knowledge with my classes, but I also learned of Him. Being outside was amazing. It was awesome to see the beautiful blue sky. I just felt good and at home with all my surroundings again.

I met a beautiful young lady at school. Her name was Rachel. She was going to school for accounting. She and I quickly hit it off and started dating. Her parents had also divorced, but had remarried. Both families were very nice to me. She lived at her mom's house. Rachel's mom was very caring, like mine. Her stepfather and I shared a common interest—stockcar racing. Rachel and I liked each other's company.

I had been going to this school for about a year and a half. The summer classes were just around the corner, and I was unsure of which classes I wanted to enroll in. I was thinking about majoring in Elementary Education. After the classes let out, I walked outside and saw a big pine tree. As I looked at that tree, nature instructed me to revive my knowledge of it a little more intensely. I very much loved nature. Don't get me wrong: kids were a big part of my life, but to see tall grass, wildflowers, wildlife, big pine and oak trees, and feel a nice breeze flowing under a big tree was great!

The next step was going straight into the registrar's office. (I felt like I had just won the lottery and was going to cash in.) A counselor called out for me. I went into her office, said hello, and started spilling the beans. I told her just what I thought about nature and forestry; she just listened and from across the desk.

Finally, she was able to search on her computer and told me about a school that had just what I wanted. It was Lake City Community College in Lake City, Florida.

Greg had been helping me by guiding me and advising me. I announced my decision to my mother and him. They both were completely supportive and happy, and they both had the highest hopes for me. After finding out everything I needed to do, I enrolled. The next thing I knew, it was time to transport myself to my new dwelling. It was just another leap to another stone. What was so cool about it was that Rachel was going to a university that was only an hour and a half away, so she and I wouldn't be far from one another.

To think that it had only been about fours years since my severe brain surgery and that I had learned everything over again was simply amazing. Going to a new college was really different for me because I never really had been that far away from home. It was simply cool. My brother-in-law helped me plant my feet. He helped me with school and my living arrangements. I got an apartment not far from the school. My brother was nice enough to bring up all my stuff, like furniture, things from my bedroom, kitchen items, and everything else.

My Christian faith, however, kind of slowed down. I was living in a brand new town, not knowing a soul, and constantly studying! By now I was kind of smart, but I had to hit the books. School was on my mind, but God was in my heart. The school was a small one and very cozy. The town was just like that too. It sure had big pine and oak trees. I liked everything about the town and was very impressed with my surroundings. I had some of my family visit just before I started, and I had to show them my college.

My cousins and I on school grounds

I had enrolled in the fall forestry classes and was ready. As I enter the classroom and sat down, it continued to fill up with students. The class was packed to the rim. There must have been thirty students or maybe more. It was obvious that studying was going to take up a good percentage of my time because the classes were long. The labs took even longer, which added to the overwhelming amount of studying I had. It was a different experience for me, and I needed that.

The forestry classes covered different abilities required to undergo most forestry practices. I only had two teachers for my whole forestry program. There names were Jim and Kurt. One of my classes was called Fire and Smoke Management. Part of this class was about weather conditions and prescribed burns. The prescribed burns were done to lower the overgrowth on plantations, allowing faster growth. Some of the class was about how the time of the year affected how a person could burn fire lines, and any solution or product that would contribute to unwanted fires.

The forestry program contained other subjects, ranging from becoming educated on a forestry computer program to ecology. My favorite class was in dendrology, the study of tree species. It was totally awesome to find out about trees. We went over the differences between the soft and hardwoods. The softwood trees had needle-like leaves. These groups of coniferous trees are called gymnosperms. The hardwood trees were deciduous trees, with broad leaves, and were called angiosperms. For part of my final, I had to hand in a large family album with a table of contents. It was packed with sixty-five different leaves (each one from a different kind of tree).

Over half the album contained leaves from hardwoods, including maples, sweetgum, river birch, and so on. The others were needle-like leaves, such as eastern redcedar, slash pine, and bald cypress.

Kurt had the students make up this album with the common, scientific, and family names of the trees. We even had to include whether the tree was of commercial importance, its habitat (wet or dry), and a short sentence telling about each tree. We studied how to grow trees; what the best habitat conditions for each kind were, either on wet or dry lands; how available their fruit was; and how to make a profit from them. In another class, we had the opportunity to learn how to cruise timber. Cruising timber was done on foot, and involved examining an area of timber (acreage or plantation), counting each tree species, estimating their diameter and height, and noting the predominant species.

After cruising, I had to use the information that I collected to draw a graph on art paper (I loved drawing), and then allow the teacher to grade it. If the cruising was done for a consumer, they would have to look over the work. If the job was performed for a real client, a profit would be made on my part for the entire land that had been cruised. This actually was our very last class, and we got the opportunity to work for a company cruising timber. I did not make much from it, but the experience was awesome.

The school had elected a president for the forestry club and I received the honor. We were involved in several events. One of the occurrences was very much up my alley.

It was working with the Special Olympics. I very much loved taking part in working with those children. On one occasion the children, school, and I where involved in track and field events. The kids would arrive (they were so adorable), and take up their positions at the starting line, ready to take off at the sound of the whistle.

When I would blow the whistle and yell "Go," they would run their little hearts out. We were giving them the opportunity to be free on their own for just a moment. You could see big smiles and positive reactions when they crossed the finish line. That was really cool. I was a big part of this. You could always tell when I got back from these events because my voice had completely given out!

At other times, the forestry club was allowed to be a part of the community. We would have a big fair with rides, games, and booths that showcased our school's programs and other formative community programs. We had a forestry booth. I had the opportunity to dress up as Smokey Bear for the children. That was absolutely fun. It was great giving hugs to the kids.

I started going to a gym and lifting weights again. I met a guy at the gym who was going to my school. He and I became friends. We would go to the gym and just hang out. I needed his friendship living in this town. Sure, there were several people I spoke to, but I did not hang out with them.

Chapter 9
Finding Myself

As I continued in school, I started to miss home. My mother often visited me, and other family members did occasionally. I sure missed my dad at times. I wished that I could have had the satisfaction of speaking to him personally, face to face, and telling him of my adventures. The little town and my adjustment to it were delightful. Several different tree species would bloom throughout this town. It was breathtaking, but only if you were a tree hugger like me. Beautiful flowers grew everywhere, and animal life was surely abundant.

Rachel and I were always either coming or going between each other's places on the weekends. It was either she or I that did the driving. It must have been my first semester, and I skipped school for the day. I didn't do this often, but I had a really good reason. I drove over to her apartment, ran up to the door, and knocked. She opened up the door and there I was, on one knee. I asked her to marry me. She said yes, we kissed, and then soon after I had to get back home.

She and I were great friends; we did everything together. We never really got upset with each other, or tired of each other's company, though we did find a fault in our relationship. The cause of the disagreement was religious differences. She wanted to stay Catholic. As you know, I was a Baptist.

I was not going back to Catholicism. I remember when we even went to get some counseling from my dearest friend, Pastor Gary. The problem was not going anywhere. So, we continued the relationship just like we did back home. We would go out in her town and do a little partying, and do the same in my town. One night did not turn out like any other.

As she and I were sleeping through the night, she awoke to a disturbing movement in our bed. She had no idea to what was going on. She called out for me, but I did not respond. Getting up and turning on a light, she witnessed me experiencing a major seizure. My entire body started shaking, my muscles were twitching, foam was coming out of my mouth, and my eyes were rolling back into my head.

She jumped to react, calling nine-one-one. Her fast reaction saved me from any other possible injury. The paramedics and doctors completed their mission. After departing from the hospital a couple of days later, my mother and I went to see a neurologist in Gainesville, Florida. He was trained in the diagnosis and treatment of nervous-system disorders. In short, the trauma resulted in my having to take medication for the rest of my life. It had been about six years since my accident. The doctor called what I had experienced a grand mal seizure.

I told him about the stress and worry I was experiencing at that time in my life. He informed me that these factors had contributed to my having a seizure. These stressors included one of my friends being shot (alcohol and another person took part in it), family, school, and my girlfriend. Just a little bit of stress. Being exposed to these facts of life had a tremendous impact on my life.

My girlfriend and I were no longer on the same path. Soon after that, she and I decided to end our relationship, but to remain committed as friends. Everything happening to me transformed the way I was to live my life. This also included the consumption of alcohol; I decided to give up alcohol, for good.

Being a single man again, I wanted to get back into a church. Studying was still a large part of my life, but now that my weekends were free, I could now use them to do what I wanted. On Sundays, I attended Baptist churches. There is one church service that I still remember today. An older preacher used the roots of a tree and the crown (branches and leaves) as a metaphor in his sermon. It was not about having the ability to see the roots dying or view the crown, branches, or the leaves turning color, but it was about the whole tree itself. He discussed the development of the whole tree and its life span, relating it to our relationship with God. It was very meaningful to me. The people in my small, country town who attended these churches were noticeable, and quite friendly. These people were not afraid to talk to you. They did not point to the sky with their noses like people at other churches back home.

Talking to God at night helped me to fall to sleep. I found complete peace through prayer. When unyielding, knotty exams had me studying more, I prayed more, if you know what I mean! Imagine the distance, passing of time, and how God has allowed me to expand and find out about this crazy, wonderful world. It was just hard to believe that I was sitting in this school, miles away my home, going for a future degree.

The phrases "Everything happens for a reason," and "Life works in mysterious ways," are not quite correct. I came to realize that these phrases were missing a word or two at the beginning. It should, "*God* lets everything happen for a reason." and "*God* works in mysterious ways." Our lives should incorporate these words in some way.

Those words helped me to reach my goal. I was complete! I had finished what I had started. On the July 29, 1998, I stood in high spirits to receive my Associate in Science Forest Management degree. Though the classes had been packed to the rim, only a few students graduated. My family on my mother's side came to witness my achievement.

It was a very special time and I felt proud of myself. My past was not going to stop me. I was able to find out my destiny with God's help, but the decision was up to me. It was as if He was handing our destiny out to us, yet we needed to be willing to accept it. To find out what our destiny may be is to understand your desires and what you want out of life.

At the same time, I decided to extend my education and get a bachelors degree in forestry. I moved down to Gainesville, Florida. Getting an apartment and enrolling at Santa Fe Community College to get my associate in arts degree had been no problem, but being back in school did seem to be a problem. I was ready to move forward, though. It was time to put my educated mind to work.

Chapter 10
Professionalism

I was equipped with a computer. After searching websites that led me to send out roughly sixty resumes to meaningful states, I waited, waited, and waited, and the phone was not ringing concerning those sixty resumes. My prayers became more intense. I found myself wanting to pull out my hair while waiting for this important phone call. As I was watching the television one day, the phone rang. The blood went straight to my head. Reaching quickly for the phone, I answered to find that the gentleman on the opposite end was from Red Lodge, Montana. He was calling from Beartooth Ranger District.

His name was Dan, and he asked if I was still interested in a job that began in May and went until August. It was a position as a forestry technician, performing the operation and maintenance of recreational facilities. After speaking to him, I asked if I could call back the next morning. He replied, "Yes."

After we ended our phone call without a pause, I quickly dialed my mother, and then my brother-in-law. Without hesitation, they and I completely agreed that I should take the job. It was overwhelming to hear their voices filled with such support.

The next morning I made a call to let this gentleman know that I would very much love to accept his offer. I was so happy, and at the same time, I felt so overwhelmed. I would be on open land for miles and miles with bewildering mountains of beauty. I saddled up my Jeep and brought a map that I had marked out for the trip. I did the math in my head. It was a forty-hour trip, give or take. Even my tires were ready for this long journey!

My loving mother was not going to let me depart by myself, so she voluntarily traveled with me. I told her that I would have to do the driving, however. It was another goal that I had to conquer. Along the way to Montana, we visited family and a friend. My mother had a friend living in New Orleans and a brother who lived in Texas. During our trip, she and I got a motel room in New Mexico. It was pretty neat in the morning because there was about an inch of snow on my truck. As we neared my destination, we started traveling along the side of the Rocky Mountains, admiring this untold beauty, this breathtaking land. I could not believe how beautiful it really was.

By now, the town was visible. There was not a traffic light in sight, only stop signs. It was early May when I arrived for my duty. A small amount of snow was still present throughout the area. Up in the higher mountains, it must have been about two feet or more. That was a tremendous sight, seeing how I loved snow. Mom and I checked in at local motel until I had to report for duty. When a storm would come across this cozy tiny town, wonderful snowflakes would come floating down.

We spent our time together absorbing the air, the surroundings, and our relationship. My mom stayed four or five days, and then she had to return home. She adored the scenery. Ninety-nine percent of the people were so tender, caring, and interested in hearing about us around this town.

It was so refreshing to be around these people whom we did not even know. Back home, it was like a rat race, where everyone is in a hurry to get were they are going, and a good percentage of them are not even friendly.

The Red Lodge's elevation was 5,555 feet above sea level. True hometown folks called the Rocky Mountains, "God's Country." It was unquestionably enjoyable to spend time with these people. I met some amazing people and fellow employees. The head district ranger was named Rand. He held down the fort. He and the others had their own job to do. I worked under a few of the guys. Dan was in charge of my position, Tom worked with fire, and Jeff was the recreation specialist. I became friends with everyone working for Beartooth Ranger District. I had the pleasure of becoming good friends with a couple of those employees and their families.

Once I started my employment, they moved me to another position, Dispersed Recreation. It must have been due to my skills and knowledge. I was good with my hands and they could see that. Roofing had become one of my projects on a small building owned by the district. Even asphalt paving was a part of these projects. My partner and I would use cold asphalt to patch areas. Rand and the other staff had put my abilities to work.

A young guy and I had to assemble these huge wooden signs for the names of national parks at their entrances. The national parks were packed to the rim with different soft and hardwood trees. Some of these trees were huge. In a way, I wished that they could speak to me. I bet they would tell a long story of the history of the Rocky Mountains. The view was simply unforgettable.

I loved driving in these mountains. Sometimes I went up to the campgrounds and collected funds at these drop off spots. I had an opportunity once to be with Tom and maintain an area that had undergone explosions to clear a path for hikers. One thing that I very much liked was being a Park Ranger on the weekends and holidays. I patrolled the parks and campsites in a new company four-by-four truck that was owned by the district. My uniform looked very professional. A friend took this picture while we were in the Pryor Mountains.

Me in uniform patrolling

It was a complete natural high, and so exciting to drive up these sharp turns and large inclines to reach my destinations. At the very top of these national parks, at different times, there were people from all over the world. They were all filled with a physical grace. I met some outstanding people with absolute inner hearts that were very peaceful. They all enjoyed nature just as I did, and had wonderful stories to tell.

I lived in a house that was just behind the ranger district. At night, I spent a good percentage of my time lying in bed reading the Bible. One time, I went to a saloon to shoot pool. As I was playing pool, I saw a customer and the bartender arguing, and later I saw them on the floor, swinging their fists, and no one was doing anything. The first thing that came to my mind was to break it up, and I did. Alcohol was very much a part of the social life in this little town, but not mine. I had realized that I did not want it in my life. I didn't want to live that way anymore.

I heard a long time ago there had been a lot more saloons here because the miners liked to drink! I was told that a disaster had happened and given directions to where the mine was located just outside of town. So I drove to the Smith Mine. When I arrived there, I read a memorial sign that said that on February 27, 1943, there had been an explosion inside the mine that killed seventy-four men from the towns Red Lodge, Bearcreek, and Washoe. They lost their lives due to concussions and gas poisoning. That must have been awful for folks who lost loved ones. My compassion goes out to those people; I know how it feels to lose loved ones.

While working at the Beartooth Ranger District, I was given the chance to arrange an event with the community's recreation center. It was a great feeling, bringing out smiles in kids. They were informed of the forest service with the help of staff members and Smokey Bear. The children really enjoyed learning about forestry, having hands-on time with the staff, and receiving hugs from this furry little friend. I really enjoyed their hugs and wearing the costume again! It was another time when I could give back what God gave to me—love.

Another awesome experience I had was having the chance to see real animals right next to me, with no walls or fences. I had the opportunity to encounter (just feet away) live bears, moose, foxes, and even wild horses! One day, I was driving up a mountain and slowed way down because a baby bear was crossing the dirt road. Another striking, absolutely forever moment was when I sat on the top of this mountain in the company's truck. I heard a sound and thought, "It can't be." All of a sudden, a family of wild horses ran up right in front of the truck! They rearranged themselves for a moment and then took off in another direction. They ran fast and furiously, as if the leader had taken control and told the others to follow his lead.

Another moment that stands out occurred when I was traveling by road. I went to the top of the Beartooth Mountains. They must have been around ten or eleven thousand feet above sea level. I was told that some peaks were taller than 12,000 feet. The mountains still had some snow on them. So, I parked my truck right between the edge of this mountain top and the side of the road.

There were only two things standing on this edge—my snowboard and I. That's when I dropped down the side of this beautiful, white mountain.

I picked up speed and enjoyed the thrill of this ride, though it shortly came to an end. After a major rush had overcome my body, I looked up to the very top. Man, as fast as I had gone down the mountain, it took me a lot longer to climb back up to the top. I had to drop down that mountain all over again because the rush was just too awesome. Forever content in my mind was being in those mountains. Just as I had been told, I realized that it was God's Country. That is where I stretched out my arms and hands to extend my gratitude and appreciation to my Savior.

Me giving praise to my Lord Jesus Christ

All of my goodbyes to all my friends in Red Lodge were carved in stone. The whole trip was sealed in my mind. I will miss my experience and time there. I had accomplished another goal, with an impression made with God's love. I learned to ask God not to come into my life, but what if I could come into His? For He already is in our lives, whether or not we know this. We are the ones who need to see and feel that God loves us. We decide whether we will be a part of His life. I had once been a partial believer only to become an extreme believer.

Conclusion
Knowing of Life Now

As this story ends, I hope you can decide your present, your future, and overcome your past. I hope that certain thoughts, actions, and your ability to react can be without resistance that might overturn your life. It meant so much to me to see the sun rise and then fall! There are some things in life that people take for granted, not knowing that this might be harmful to them or hurt a loved one in their life.

The next day can go anywhere or be extraordinary. We really do not know. I am thankful to be a part of daily living. Accidents happen, but having God present in our lives is the only way good can accrue from it. Losing a loved one can mean the world, if not more, but there is a thought behind it. The doors in our lives open and close. The opportunity is present in your life if you have the door opened towards Him.

It maybe unfortunate to see unknown roads for you along the way, but just making a turn could point you in the right direction. It is best *not* to have something so influential, like my brain surgery, to make you into a different person. God sees the person you are trying to be. When the moment is right, God takes control. Strive is the word to use, when thinking of an alternative.

A long time ago, a young lady told me that life is faith. Faith is complete trust, and trust gives you the ability to succeed, which makes you strive.

I live my life now with a whole different perspective. My experiences have forced me to move one hundred and eighty degrees the opposite direction. The impact of past obstacles in no way can evenly match the strong arm that I now possess. Drinking alcohol, fighting, treating girls differently and not caring that much, and being the same size as the earth was just an act. The past actions I performed were only because of me. The result of a major accident that intensively altered my life was unthinkable. It is a great wonder for God to see me as incredible and for you to see me as normal.

I had to learn this. Look at what I accomplished. It was not present at first, but slowly I realized what it was. The Lord our God is here. All you have to do is walk the right path. He sees. He hears. He speaks. I am not saying that He will reply immediately, but he will when He sees that you are ready! Then He allows you to take steps forward when you are in need. God does works in mysterious ways. I can tell you from experience. I hope that my desire might provoke you or someone you know to find some type comfort. Confidentially, it has in mine. I must be thankful and respect my past.

Some people might be generous in forgiving you, but the only one who counts no matter what is God. He is the light at the end of the tunnel that we need. I personally found out about how Jesus can forgive us for our sins and mistakes.

The way I live now cannot even be matched by a single thing, not even the world. It has opened my eyes to a newer, reviving style of living. It has also brought a whole new approach to living my life in which I am so, so, so happy, and thankful to the people who gave me assistance along the way. My caring, thoughtfulness, heartwarming, giving, and love has expanded enormously.

God gave me a second chance—a second chance at a life with a purpose. I believe that He has seen my character. I believe He has seen my personality. I believe that He has seen my possibilities. Also, I believe that He has seen the way children affect my life. Seeing this showed Him that I could be a person who could make a difference. God answered all the prayers before, during, and after my accident. Devoting my life to Him and realizing who He is has made me into a better person. I realize now that I have been granted life, humanity. I believe that He had to step back until I was ready for Him.

After this whole experience from beginning to end, and the years I spent waiting to write this book, my life has become so impressive. I used my knowledge to expand my ability to expand this gift of life. This gift outlines many of my achievements. One of these had to do with my career in forestry and educating children and the public. I became a recreation leader for a nature center and park in Largo, Florida. I very much enjoyed teaching them about nature and wildlife.

I found great satisfaction through educating children and the public about how nature takes its course, and about different animals.

My love for Jesus opened my heart to educating children more about history and the present time. Pathways Community Church was exactly what I wanted and needed.

The church was small, and people there were just like the ones in that tiny, cozy town up in the mountains. I became good friends with the pastors, especially the children's pastor. His name was Dave. I cherished working with children. This provoked in me a desire for higher education, which led me to a Youth Ministry bachelor's degree from St. Petersburg Theological Seminary.

Ever since my accident, one my dreams was to have children of my own. Now, I was trying to find a woman who believed in and found interest in Jesus. I wanted this so dearly. I was searching and searching to meet that very special woman who could join me in this. I searched near and far, going out of my way for years, trying to find that woman. I did meet several amazing women only to find out that they did not meet my approval. I had been praying to God for a very long time for this to take place. Only now can I see that He was not ready.

God works in mysterious ways. He had her right underneath my nose, and I did not even know it. I was living in this condo complex. I had seen this woman occasionally and would speak to her. It was November 2004; one evening, Margaret and I stopped to talk. She asked me if I would like to meet her daughter, Lisa. I replied that I would, but personally I thought she was going to be like the other women I had met.

Margaret said that they would come over later that evening. By this time, the evening had turned into night. Suddenly, there was a knock on my door. I went to the door, opened it, and that was it. God had placed her right in front of me. After dating her for only five weeks, I had to ask Lisa if she would become my wife.

About a year later, we both wore our wedding rings, showing gratitude toward Jesus Christ. She said, "A prayer went out also to meet that special Christian man." What's really strange about this whole picture is that I learned that our mothers had known each other for a short time, and that my mother had even met Lisa once a long time ago. They had lost contact until Lisa and I got together.

As for my relationship with the Lord, He has once again answered my prayers. He gave me a special baby girl and an adorable step-son. When my wife had become pregnant, and until my daughter was born, I talked to my Lord Jesus Christ, asking for my baby to be fully healthy and strong, and He absolutely answered.

Me, Sebastian, Lisa, and Lakoda

Whatever happens in our lives, it's always positive to have God present. The result of this is that you will not have to worry about the outcome and what the future will be. He answers the prayers that we hand over to Him, bad or good. Whatever is bad will always, always (depending on His time) turn out to be good. The results of prayers might not be what we want, yet they are ultimately what we need! This is the destiny He has for, in, and around us.

The life that I lived in the past was nothing of consequence, and the direction I was heading in was unfortunate. Yet, you have to overcome your causes to be. The giving is here and encounters a life ultimately in His hands. This path has fundamentally transcended boundaries, only to become stable. I wish that the people of this world could be more willing to love and ask for the help of our Lord Jesus Christ. To believe in a given, everlasting opportunity can only be *My Miracle*.

This is your opportunity to open up to the world and let others know about your experience that altered your life. And, how this encounter has rearranged your life for the greater good.

www.sharingmiracles.net